The Art of
What You Can't Touch

Ewen Glass
abuddhapress@yahoo.com

ISBN: 9798339827511

Ewen Glass 2024
®™©
Alien Buddha Press 2024

Now with FREE worksheet!!!!!

Cerumen Kid

Nights (whispered)

Our generation of the coloured noise,
of ASMRtists and
the salival clack of empires.
BetterHelp better help,
or forward to thunder
and Krakatoa and
Tunguska event,
so that, in time,
we all might hear nothing
but something else.

My Family Fostered

The boy who killed the kittens was cute. His face was open, ceramic pale, freckled. He knew what to say sometimes; other times he would light matches under his bed like the troubled kid in a Nineties thriller.

Twenty years later, I google him and find a series of local news stories. As an adult, he was charged with dangerous driving, then contempt of court then–

We had to wrap him in his own BraveStarr duvet to stop him from hurting us. As a teenager I held his legs, my Mum his top half. Eventually he'd sweat it out and I could go back to my room and lock my door. I'm relieved not to find anything worse online, but I want to see his face so I look him up on Facebook.

He seems to change his profile pic a lot. Still good-looking. And then I see the banner photo– our cat Pepper had a small litter and he killed most of them. No kick, no spasm of anger, Mum found him staring into one's eyes as he strangled it.

She took the remaining kittens to the vet and I was left at home, listening to him bang about in his room like he'd been wronged. Now I look at his proud smile in the photo.

I look at his arm draped lovingly around a chocolate Labrador's neck. And I'm worried for it. And him. And me.

Maybe he's just not a cat person.

Uncle's Birthday of Hummingbirds

Liver-breached words: 'it's just my truth what can you say to that? What manner of hummingbird are you that you can't sit still?

I'll have my life in small plates discussed and shared or I dunno messy and discarded? A group of hummingbirds is a bouquet,

funny coz they used to think hummingbirds couldn't smell.' Bile ducts blocked, his skin has jaundiced quickly; knowing enough of

what's to come, the guests let him talk, ignoring that he looks like a highlighter to accept his version of celebration before –

That Time I Got So Scared I Thought

I could die, and in softest-sounding Pudsey too, once the biggest village in UK. It was a close night, summer like gauze over terraced houses, the moon spotting through. My bedroom window was open and I soon fell asleep, *Keep The Aspidistra Flying* flat beside me. A scream breaks across my face. I hurry to piece together the dark, my heart beating Looney-Tunes fast. More shouting! There's a shadow on my head, getting bigger… a falling anvil. Instinct rolls them out – will the people outside hurt each other? will they hurt someone else? are they out for blood?! – but it's just a couple and now they're kissing and saying how stupid it all was. Their voices felt Right Beside Me, but it's the quality of the light in my room that worries me, the streetlight just outside my window— the anvil hits me. More percussive than concussive. But try as I might, I can't keep the floor from cracking beneath my feet and I plummet into the living-room below. I look right at you as this floor begins to crack too. *Gulp*. Crashing into the basement, I keep going and keep going, following through layers of mantle and core onto the roof of my childhood house, through neglected slate into shared attic bedrooms and further, into the familiar light/dark of my childhood bedroom. There's a shadow on his face and he looks at me. The floorboards give way and I finally land on the ground-floor, groping for breath.

Only now do I feel the cool press of cast-steel on my guts. The lights are on down here, a TV murmuring away, while up in my bedroom, he's lookng at me and there's a shadow on his face. The moon? A Streetlight? Trapped, I open my book and read about poor old Gordon Comstock again, as I absently finger indented words on the anvil. I swear, if this says ACME...

When Dancing is Semaphore

I'm the red flag.
My message? Should've eaten more
Now I'm calling from a bubble,
beside other bubbles.
Mitosis on the dance floor.
If I'm communicating from a distance,
she's a stye. We kiss.
Jaeger flab in mouths.
She says her Mum died –
I don't know what to say so I pretend I don't hear,
but I need clarity. When?
This Morning. She looks at her watch.
I guess yesterday morning now.
She asks if we can go somewhere and –
I feel lightheaded, all at sea,
my conscience gesticulating.
I ask if she wants to talk about her Mum or –
she sighs and starts grinding against someone else.
I leave to flag down a taxi.

Litter/Foster Brother

Safety-pin ribs, and black-rice eyes.
Ungenerous fur; mottled red
is the blanket box where placenta lay,
a feast of preservation. Failed.
An eight year-old snaps safety-pins closed.
Eyes flower, and against
Great Natural Law #311, shrink
through seed to nothing.
Or a purse discarded on the floor,
beside three others.

Mild Steel and Granda

How dense that muscle
playful fathers pinch
to touch their sons

(nape)

and students paint moony
futures in lectures

(nucha).

She touched him there,
dancing in Betty Staffs, then –
a kiss as careless as the decades after.
Tired of curating oblivion,
she left before his
skin split like syllables,
on a hot rad-i-a-tor.
No jig, nor flight, nor fall,
he on-ly re-clined one night

(a pain in the neck!
Barely felt)

into the black of our im-a-gined sib-i-lance

(*hiss*
or
sssh;
take your pick).

Place Setting

Hash.
Hessian.
Create a table
for us to sit

                in lines,

cross-
hatched pauses,
discrete as numbers,
levied fair (whole)

on
all diners.
Render a stalemate
in patterns or,

                in time,

ask
by breached bone,
whether cell-by-cell
means together

and
side-by-side
apart. More Sunday
lunches in March

        and rhymes

that
have to be
met more than half-way,
or — not at all.

At Forty

	pissing
the	bed
is	portent
of	prostate
or	bladder
	problems
or	possibly
and	purely
a	past that scares you so much you you
	piss
the	bed

Placing in a competition

brought me up to Scotland,
and to Argyll to see my dad.
After a lunch of sausages,
I waited for an early bus out.
He hugged me, put his head
on my chest for a moment;
is it right then that saying,
parents become children?
There was a rainbow so low
across the loch I thought
it was a seaside attraction.
I saw three more on the way
home on the bus, and knew
I wouldn't see him again,
my child.

Clean Bean

Self-Care

Only when plucking nose-hair do I think I have synaesthesia: turmeric fireworks, or good Hungarian paprikash perhaps; washing bottles for recycling, balsamic waves fetched by shaking; heat; the substance of stars. I brace for a tiny death each hair, only to be denied grace when – exposed, eyes wet – I sneeze and my urethral sphincter contracts. For a moment my entire body is a single fold in space. Never more abstract. Never more corporeal.

And my partner calls me dramatic.

Teams

The water isn't quite brack.
Brack*ish* maybe.
Estuary humour,
common as sandpipers
on shop signs.
By The Crown, smokers mock
barrel-and-twine boats
crossing the narrows under yoke of
corporate camaraderie.

And look at these absolute clowns!

Arranged in lines,
a team in black searches sod and sediment.
They aren't with OffLimitSolutions
and there's no novelty mug;
theirs is a prize of tissue and bloat.
The kind heave of the water
has pushed
and pulled the body,
ashore and back out.
The officers reach for him,
and the smokers are suddenly reverent

For goodness sake,

one says,

Can nothing bob solemnly?!

Questions Fom A Reporter Outside the Courthouse on the Nature of Justice

1. Sir, sir, do you think justice was served today?

2. Sir? Sir? Do you think- Sir?

3. Sir? Sir? Do-

4. Sir? Sir? Sir, excuse me-

5. Sir, do you think- sir?

6. Sir? Sir?

7. Sir? Sir? Sir? Sir? Sir? Sir? Sir?

8. Sir? Sir? Sir? Sir? Sir? Sir?

9. Sir? Sir? Sir!

10. Sir?

The Cinema Experience Is Here To Stay

As is the fashion, I went to a 4D cinema.
My seat thrummed and tilted; I was immersed
so I gave 5D a try. A similar deal but there's more
under the bonnet. You're thrummed, tilted *and* jolted.
Immersive!
Before long the call of 6 Ds was too strong. It's a fine
thing smelling explosions.
Catching a matinee at my local 7D, I *felt* the heat,
but it wasn't enough.
I travelled to an 8D cinema in Tillicoultry.
to be touched by hands and lips and –
I confess I was chasing the dragon now,
right into that new 9D place in Monmouthshire.
I got to choose the ending of the film!
There were more creative choices to be made with
10D technology; one could, for instance, toggle
between male gaze mode and male gaze mode.
Then there's the 11D, where you get a line
in the movie, usually something simple
like 'the sauteed scallops' or 'phone-call, maam'.
12D begins before the shoot. You download
Final Draft, take numerous notes-calls and try
to solve second act problems.
The 13D cinema on the isle of Easdale presented
A new approach. I became deeply aware of bacteria

crawling over my face.
I heard a rumour that 14D cinema involved building four IMAX screens in your guts,
so I went straight to the cutting-edge 15D theatre in Fordwich.
The film seemed poor at first. Talk about passive characters!
But then I realised the actors were looking at me:
I was the movie.
Feeling altogether too self-conscious, I didn't know how to act.
Natalie Portman was the first to boo.
Kevin Hart got a few cheap laughs at my expense.
Gerard Butler just seemed desperately desperately sad.
It was horrible.

Chelonoidis Carbonaria / Red-Footed Tortoise

His face a collage around black eyes. Shares of autumn titivate legs, but there's warning in his dropped tail so I set him down. He shits on bark. Unchanged for a hundred million years, his family knew dinosaurs. I know Microsoft Teams. Moments borrowed between meetings keep us in touch, he with history, me with maintenance, and I evangelise often to friends: in scientific experiments, tortoises learn to use touchscreens faster than dogs. Or grandparents ha ha. He took a chunk out of my big toe once; if it wasn't a strawberry before it was after. He buries his face in a piece of watermelon, adding yet more colour to his face. As the sun appears I do it – I push my scheduled meeting out of the way – and take him outside to bask, both of us to bask.

I Pity Keats

He did not know the exquisite joy of writing at soft-play.
Warehouse din and half coffee;
bacteria on rubber composites.
What image might he have conjured from screaming just screaming?
Perhaps he would have taken his shoes off and
struggled, half bent, past attentive netting
to find his son crying
and, overcome with rage,
found the boys who called him names,
only to retreat when he saw how hard their Dads looked.
Maybe Keats would have done that.

Get Off My Lawn &
While You're Doing So Don't Judge Me

When punk – and I use these words advisedly – ass teenagers look with pity or disdain on the middle-aged, they might say I don't want to get old and fat like them, thinking perhaps that old and fat are the same thing, or that gradual weight gain comes from a turgid, settled life. Well, it just about makes me want to shake those little punk asses. There's no complacency here, nor a paucity of imagination. If there's a lack of thought it's by design, a balm to the competitive chafe of logistics, roads not taken and that worrying velvet catkin on my testicle; I guess Olympic catastraphizing is nothing. Just how could middle-aged spread speak of comfort when we are so full of demons? Don't you think they're hungry?!

When Will You Stop Hugging Me?

I borrow you from the ground and hold you laughing until oh I'm the dirty rascal now and soon you won't let me touch your neck or stroke your hair much less lift you towards sky when you are taller than me and between cradles and graves we have such love whether we're in arms or continent we have such love and if we're counting down in years now so be it but I'll warn you son I'm bad at maths

FREE worksheet!!!!!

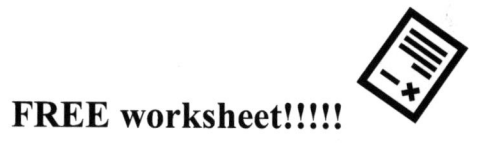

Please answer all questions:

1. Improbable pheasant
   at the back door –

                        Should I befriend it? _____

2. Convoluted recipe for a
   Spanish flan –

                        Should I make it? _____

3. Destructive patterns
   from my childhood –

                        Should I break them? _____

4. It's so bloody easy being
   positive when it's not you –

                        isn't it? _____

5.

                      Isn't it??????!!!!!   _____

6. Ill-advised outburst
     against imagined reader –

                    Should I retract it?   _____

Previously Published Work

My Family Fostered – Gordon Square Review / That Time I Got So Scared I Thought – Bridge Eight / When Dancing is Semaphore – Bicoastal Review / Litter/Foster Brother – Okay Donkey / Place Setting – Winged Penny Review / At Forty – Grey Hands Literary Magazine / Placing in a competition – HAD / Self-Care – Cathexis Northwest Press / Teams – Paddler Press / Questions From A Reporter – Magazine1 / The Cinema Experience Is Here to Stay – Full Mood Mag / Chelonoidis Carbonaria – Pinhole Poetry / I Pity Keats – Dreich Magazine / Get Off My Lawn - Maudlin House / When Will You Stop Hugging Me – Club Plum Literary / Worksheet – Voidspace

Ewen Glass (he/him) is a screenwriter and poet from Northern Ireland who lives with two dogs, a tortoise and lots of self-doubt; on a given day, any or all of these can be snapping at his heels. His poetry has appeared or is forthcoming in Okay Donkey, HAD, Poetry Scotland, Gordon Square Review, and elsewhere. On socials (and indeed in real life) he is pretty much ewenglass everywhere.

Printed in Great Britain
by Amazon